Defenders of the short-sighted men who in their greed and selfishness will, if permitted, rob our country of half its charm by their reckless extermination of all useful and beautiful wild things sometimes seek to champion them by saying that "the game belongs to the people." So it does; but not merely to the people now alive, but to the unborn people. The "greatest good for the greatest number" applies to the number within the womb of time, compared to which those now alive form but an insignificant fraction. Our duty to the whole, including the unborn generations, bids us to restrain an unprincipled present-day minority from wasting the heritage of those unborn generations. The movement for the conservation of wild life, and the larger movement for the conservation of all our natural resources, are essentially democratic in spirit, purpose and method.

Theodore Roosevelt, "Bird Reserves at the Mouth of the Mississippi," in A Book-Lover's Holidays in the Open, Charles Scribner's Sons, New York, 1916.

THE MURAL PROJECT

Photography by

ANSEL ADAMS

Selected and with an introduction by

PETER WRIGHT & JOHN ARMOR

REVERIE PRESS

SANTA BARBARA

1989

to
those who maintain and preserve
the national forests and parks

The assistance of the officers, staff and curators of the National Archives is gratefully acknowledged, in addition to their preservation of the original Ansel Adams prints that were used in this book.

Quotes on frontispiece and page 20 reprinted with permission of Charles Scribner's Sons, an imprint of Macmillan Publishing Company from "A Book Lover's Holidays in the Open" by Theodore Roosevelt. Copyright 1916 Charles Scribner's Sons; Copyright renewed 1944 by Edith K. Carow Roosevelt.

THE MURAL PROJECT photography by ANSEL ADAMS
Copyright © 1989 by Reverie Press, a division of Day Dream Publishing Inc.

Published by Reverie Press, a division of Day Dream Publishing Inc., 212 Cottage Grove Avenue, Santa Barbara, California 93101.

First Edition, March 1989
Library of Congress Catalog Card Number: 88-51712
International Standard Book Number: 1-55824-162-0

Preface

In 1935, Secretary of the Interior Harold Ickes conceived the idea of having murals painted on the walls of a new museum for the Department of the Interior in Washington. Many of those murals were painted and became prime tourist attractions. But in 1937 the Secretary became aware of the work of a young photographer, Ansel Adams, who was taking pictures in the National Parks of the West, especially in Yosemite, one of the earliest parks.

In time, he saw more of Adams' work, and met him. Secretary Ickes decided that some of the murals should be photographs rather than paintings. He decided that Adams was the man to take those photographs.

In October 1941, Secretary Ickes had Ansel Adams employed as an outside consultant to provide a definitive series of photographs of the National Parks, the Indians, and certain other locales such as Boulder Dam, for the Department of the Interior. A year later, by November 1942, Ansel Adams had sent 225 prints to the Department.

The quality of this series of photographs confirms the judgment of Secretary Ickes in hiring Adams for the Project. No one has ever captured the majesty of the National Parks better than Adams.

However, due to the outbreak of World War II, the Mural Project was never finished. None of these photographs were ever made into wall-sized murals as intended. The signed original prints went into storage in Washington, the negatives into storage in the vault at Yosemite National Park. Only a small number of people have even been aware that this series of photographs was taken.

Now, in this book, the heart of this collection is made available to the general public. The vision that Ansel Adams had of the National Parks of the West, the vision that Secretary Ickes believed this young photographer possessed, is now available for all to appreciate.

It is appropriate that quotations from Theodore Roosevelt accompany these photographs. He was an accomplished naturalist and writer before he became President of the United States. As President, he added millions of acres to the National Parks, Forests and Monuments of the United States. He also steadfastly championed the creation of the National Park Service. Repeatedly in his annual messages to Congress, he urged the passage of a bill to establish the Park Service. And after he left office, he continued to speak and write forcefully on the subject.

The National Park Service was finally established in 1916. But the success of that effort, whose fruits are enjoyed today by more than 300 million visitors every year, is owed to Teddy Roosevelt more than any other single person.

It is unfortunate that sometimes great achievements do not become known until those who created them have died. The excellence of these photographs is due to the genius of Ansel Adams, a dear friend for nearly five decades. But the fact that the photographs exist is due to the foresight of Secretary Ickes, who commissioned Adams for the Mural Project.

It is now 46 years after these photographs were intended to go on public display. But the power of the photographs, like the majesty of the parks themselves, is timeless. I am pleased to share in the completion of a process that Secretary Ickes and Ansel Adams began so long ago.

William Penn Mott, Jr.
Director, National Park Service
Washington, D.C.
November 18, 1988

Introduction

Most great artists do not achieve the level of recognition and success that is their due within their lifetimes. Ansel Adams, certainly one of the great photographers, perhaps the best in history, did both. And the reason is not simply that he lived and worked to the age of eighty-two. In his forties he had earned both the respect of his peers and of the public, as well as substantial commercial success.

The artists whose careers are exceptions to the rule that full acceptance of their work comes only with time, and usually after death, share a common characteristic. They possess a special talent for finding and seizing opportunities to demonstrate their craft. They know how to cultivate the patrons who can offer them unique opportunities. In the hands of these few great artists, commissions which would produce merely decorative results in the hands of lesser practitioners become masterpieces of all time.

The Mural Project was conceived by Secretary of the Interior Harold Ickes in 1935 as a series of paintings, or perhaps photographs (although at the time photographs were not considered to be sufficiently "artistic" in many quarters) to be placed on the walls of a new museum for the Department of the Interior.

Almost by accident, Ansel Adams heard about this project. In a pattern highly reminiscent of Michelangelo pursuing commissions at the Vatican, Adams pursued the Mural Project and made it his own.

The commission that Michelangelo had really wanted from Pope Julius II was to build the Pontiff's tomb, larger and more elaborate than any tomb constructed since the height of the Roman Empire. The artist made many trips to Rome to meet with Julius II. The plans were approved; the marble quarried. But there the project stalled, due to intrigue by the Pope's architect, an artistic rival of Michelangelo. So Michelangelo returned to Florence.

In August 1506, Julius II called for Michelangelo to meet with him in Bologna, where the Pope had just subdued a rival by force of arms. The artist complied and created a bronze statue of Julius in that city. Then Michelangelo was called to Rome and offered the commission for the Sistine Chapel ceiling, receiving the contract on May 10, 1508. At first he sought to decline the offer, saying that he was a sculptor, not a painter. But Julius II insisted, and four years later the masterpiece was unveiled. There is even evidence that Michelangelo's rivals engineered the commission for him, knowing he could not refuse it and expecting him to fail. The tomb that the artist wanted to execute was never built. A much altered, much smaller version was finally constructed 27 years later.

Ansel Adams had no such problems with conflicting projects. There was only one project, and he wanted it. From the time he first heard about the Mural Project, he recognized that it was the precise assignment that he sought. It represented a once-in-a-lifetime opportunity for him to shoot definitive photographs of the national parks. And he recognized that Secretary Ickes controlled the project personally, its planning, its budgets, its contents. If Adams was to get this assignment, it would be for one reason only: because he had gained the personal confidence of Harold Ickes.

Adams wanted to do this project in his own way and in his own time, but he avoided the fatal mistake of being the temperamental artist. Carefully and skillfully, step by step, he courted Secretary Ickes as Michelangelo had courted Pope Julius II. By November 3, 1941, the Mural Project belonged to Ansel Adams.

The first hard evidence of the Mural Project is a letter in May 1935, from the Treasury Department to Secretary of the Interior, Harold Ickes, about the reservation of "$110,000 for arts and decorations in the [Department's] new building." At this point, Secretary Ickes knew what he wanted; but as yet the young photographer from Yosemite and San Francisco, Ansel Adams, knew nothing about the project and had no part in it.

There was, however, one possible connection between Adams and Ickes. In 1928, Adams had married Virginia Best in Yosemite National Park. Her father operated Best's Studio in the Park. At first, Ansel and Virginia ran the photographic studio for her father, and later, as her father's health declined, Adams took it over.

Because it operated on park property, the rates it charged to the public had to be approved by the Department of the Interior.

In 1939, for instance, Best's Studio was allowed to charge 35 cents to develop a roll of 35-millimeter film, and 5 cents each for prints. The largest print that Adams made, 16x20, cost $2.50, with mounting extra. The books of the Studio were provided to justify the prices. In the years 1930 to 1938, the Studio made a profit only once and had an average loss of $1,496.85 per year, which Adams made up from his own studio in San Francisco.

Although this information came from the files of the Secretary of the Interior, matters as mundane as the price of photographs in a single park did not come to his attention. Recommendations were made by the Director of the National Park Service to the Undersecretary of the Interior. Copies of the approvals, however, were sent to Secretary Ickes' office.

In any case, the record shows that the work of Ansel Adams had come to the personal attention of Secretary Ickes by 1937. On January 6, the Acting Director of the National Park Service, A. E. Demaray, wrote a Memorandum to First Assistant Secretary Burlew, replying to an inquiry about the price of a "photographic screen for the Secretary's office." The price was $300, a handsome sum for any example of the then-young art of photography. The screen came from a gallery in San Francisco. The photographer was Ansel Adams.

The Memorandum also demonstrates that Adams understood the importance of offering courtesies to those in high places. It says, "Mr. Adams discussed the matter with Mr. Courvoisier [Adams' agent and owner of the gallery] and. . . agreed to a special price of $250" for the Department. There were two immediate responses to this memo. The Secretary mentioned that the wife of the publisher of the

Washington Post would also like a screen at the same price. And Demaray asked whether he might meet with Burlew and Adams while the latter was visiting Washington to discuss the possible employment of Adams "to do a photomural in the new building." At this point there was only the possibility that Adams might do one or a few photographs to go along with the work being done by other artists for the Mural Project series.

There would be many false starts before the assignment would actually be made, but the attention of the Secretary was now focused on the work of Ansel Adams. The day before this Memorandum was written, Secretary Ickes had expressed his wish "to view the photographic murals in his office today."

Ansel Adams met and corresponded with various subordinates of the Secretary, both at the Department of the Interior and in the Park Service. He obtained smaller, specialized assignments for the Park Service. He sent copies of some of his books, as they were published, to Secretary Ickes. By degrees, he found out what the Secretary had in mind for the Mural Project, but as yet he had no opportunity to meet Ickes and to make his proposal that he take a complete series of photographs in the Western parks.

First Assistant Secretary Burlew was the staff person whose principal duty was to make sure that the wishes and intentions of Secretary Ickes were carried out with dispatch. Serious progress toward the assignment came in a letter from Burlew on June 10, 1941, to Adams at the Museum of Modern Art in New York. It asked for a meeting, at Adams' convenience, with Ickes and Burlew. Adams recognized opportunity when he saw it. He replied by return mail and included the polite inquiry, "Not knowing the subject of the conference I shall be unable to make any preparation for discussion in advance of the meeting. . . ."

This request bore immediate fruit. Burlew wrote back to define the subject—in part because of "the very beautiful screen" that was now in the Secretary's office, the Mural Project would be on the agenda.

By August 10, Adams had a three-page, single-spaced outline of a definitive photographic treatment of the national parks in the mail to Burlew. In it he explained his approach to the project: "Negatives from which the murals will be made should all be of consistent quality. A unified aesthetic point of view is of the utmost importance. A photograph, because of its intense realism, must be completely accurate in mood and factual relationships."

There was a flurry of letters and telegrams about the exact dates of the meetings in Washington and the costs of Adams' train fare and expenses. In late August, the first meeting finally took place.

As a result of the meetings, Secretary Ickes was satisfied that some of the murals for the walls of the new museum would be photographs taken by Ansel Adams. It was agreed that Adams would be employed at the highest rate then paid to consultants for the government, $22.22 per day, and that his expenses should be reimbursed, including train fare and car mileage, at 4 cents a mile. It was to be a nonbid, sole-source contract. Burlew was delegated to get it done.

By September 30, Adams had received authority from Secretary Ickes to begin the assignment at government expense. Ickes wrote Adams a letter of introduction which said, in part, "Mr. Adams should be given every possible opportunity to take photographs of scenery and structures of reclamation projects, Indian reservations, national parks, and other places under the jurisdiction of this Department." This letter would assure Adams full cooperation from all Interior and Park employees, anywhere in the country.

In the meantime, Burlew was pushing the Civil Service Commission to approve the contract to Adams. After several strong letters in which he made it clear that the Secretary wanted it done with dispatch, the contract was approved and signed on November 3, 1941, but back-dated to October 14.

Because of Adams' meticulous record-keeping, mostly in order to prepare his periodic requests for payment of expenses, it is possible to establish not only where and when his photographs were taken, but also where and when they were processed and printed. With the declaration of war in December 1941, it was clear that all non-essential government projects would be set aside at the end of the fiscal year, June 30, 1942. Adams wrote to Burlew on December 28, 1941, suggesting that the completion of the Mural Project would be an appropriate contribution to the war effort, saying, "I believe my work relates most efficiently to an emotional presentation of 'what we are fighting for'...." This effort was not successful.

By the end of that fiscal year, Adams had taken most of the photographs he wanted, except that the war had made it impossible for him to visit and photograph Alaska. He still had many of the prints to make, however, and funds had dried up. After some negotiations with Burlew, it was agreed that Adams would stay on as a consultant to Interior, with expenses paid but with no salary, in order to make the prints.

By November 5, 1942, Adams had finished and sent to the Department of the Interior one complete set of exhibition prints of all photographs in the Mural Project. There was a total of 225. As described later, the negatives were deposited in the vault at Yosemite National Park. As a result of World War II, the Mural Project was shelved for the duration. It is impos-

sible to tell why the project was not picked up again after the war. There were certainly appropriate places in Washington where Adams' magnificent photographs could have been displayed to good effect.

Harold Ickes left office as Secretary of the Interior on February 15, 1946. There is a common syndrome in government that the "pet projects" of any major official become orphans when a new person takes over. This might explain why the Department of the Interior did not, after the war, take up the Mural Project again. But the result was that a major body of work by one of the greatest photographers of all time simply sat on a shelf and gathered dust.

Adams may have had a personal reason for not wanting the project to go forward as of 1946. As he toured the country on the government payroll and at government expense, he shot two sets of photographs, not one. His detailed records indicate that the time and expenses of shooting the mural photographs represented about half his work during this period. As he wrote in his letter to Burlew on September 30, 1941, "If I come across exciting material that I would want for personal use I will photograph it on my personal film. It will be a simple matter to keep material accounts straight."

The second set of photographs that Adams kept for himself are not identical to those from the Mural Project. They can be distinguished from the Mural Project photographs by the differing angles at which they were taken and differing patterns of light, clouds, and water surfaces.

By 1946, Adams was nationally recognized for the quality and power of his parks photographs, mostly in Yosemite, but in other locales as well. His work had become a commercial as well as an artistic success. He may have wanted to avoid competing with himself.

The photographs in the Mural Project series belonged to the government; they were available to anyone who ordered copies, with no restriction on their use. Ansel Adams may not have wanted to push for completion of the Mural Project after the war, causing those images to be hung as wall-sized prints.

Adams had used the Mural Project to hone his craft to a high art. Perhaps the best-known single photographic image ever made is the haunting scene of a moonrise over an adobe church, with a graveyard in the foreground. This photograph, entitled "Moonrise, Hernandez, New Mexico," was shot on October 31, 1941, while Adams was traveling from Mesa Verde National Park in Colorado, to Santa Fe, New Mexico, as part of the Mural Project assignment. The reason he took only one shot of this scene is demonstrated by the nature of the image. A bright whitewash of light spills over the front of the church and edges the crosses in the graveyard. The highlights are produced by the rim of the sun, which was setting behind Adams as he topped a ridge, saw the scene, and hurriedly stopped his car to take the picture. He lacked even the time to find and use his exposure meter.

The power of the Mural Project photographs is similar to that of "Moonrise, Hernandez, New Mexico," taken as they were at the same time in Adams' career. The prints in this book have been made with techniques that Adams developed later in his life, as demonstrated by his later prints of "Moonrise."

The Mural Project photographs were rediscovered by accident—an accident born of thorough research. In 1988, the authors were researching their previous book *Manzanar*, about the Japanese-American internment camps in the United States during World War II. The book contains 100 documentary photographs taken at Manzanar (one of the ten intern-

ment camps) by Ansel Adams. These photographs were located in the Library of Congress.

The Mural Project photographs were not in the Library of Congress, nor were they catalogued in its "Masters of Photography" collection. However, in a staff file there, the authors found a 2½-page listing of the Mural Project photographs, which were in storage at the National Archives. The Project was also referred to in the wartime personal correspondence file of Secretary Ickes, which had been declassified at their request for use on *Manzanar.*

There was sufficient information to locate the photographs in the National Archives. Also found there was the correspondence showing that the Department of the Interior, having no further use for the photographs, turned them over to Archives on June 8, 1962.

In order to track down the contract under which Ansel Adams worked for $22 a day, plus expenses, Adams' personnel file as a government employee was located in a warehouse in St. Louis, Missouri. In it was a wealth of information, including much of the correspondence between Adams and Burlew, and Adams' day-by-day account of the taking of these photographs. Other records came from the personal files of Secretary Ickes and from the Department of the Interior.

The records are so detailed that we know Adams insisted on using a particular film and paper in this assignment, and that he specified what he wanted so it would appear on the "approved" list for government supplies.

With the photographs and the story behind the Mural Project now becoming public knowledge for the first time, there remains one final mystery. What the Department of the Interior turned over to National Archives in 1962 were only Adams' signed prints of these photographs. As of August 18, 1942, Adams stated in a letter to Burlew that the negatives were "to be stored... in the Yosemite National Park Administration office vault," to remain "the property of the U.S. Government," and in an unusual arrangement, to have prints made from them "only by [Ansel Adams] or under his direction" during his lifetime. In short, Adams retained artistic control of this project even though it hung in abeyance for forty years.

As for the fate of the negatives, the trail ends there, in the vault at Yosemite in 1942. They are no longer in the vault. Whether the negatives have been lost or destroyed, or whether they still exist but have been misfiled somewhere, remains a mystery. The curators of Yosemite's files have pursued the issue but have reached a dead end.

Adams made signed exhibition prints of all the photographs in the Mural Project. The photographs in this book have been made from those original Adams prints. The style in which they have been reproduced is that used by Adams in the maturity of his career—high contrast, deep blacks, and bright whites—to bring out the drama of the lighting in each scene.

In presenting the photography of Ansel Adams, a major challenge is finding words that are worthy of his images. We believe it is most appropriate to use quotations from Theodore Roosevelt together with Adams' photographs. Teddy Roosevelt was a passionate lover of the vigorous life, and the outdoor life. He was an accomplished naturalist and a dedicated conservationist, as well as an excellent writer about these subjects. It is especially appropriate that Roosevelt's words accompany Adams' photographs of American Indians. Roosevelt traveled widely in Indian territory, and sat many times in tribal council meetings. There is evidence that his dedication to preserving wilderness areas was strongly influenced by his contact with native Americans.

But most importantly, Teddy Roosevelt added millions of acres to the national parks during his administration. He championed the cause of creating a single National Park Service to manage and preserve those parks until Congress finally passed the bill. In short, more than any other individual, Teddy Roosevelt helped to create and preserve the parks that Adams celebrates in his photographs.

In the captions to the photographs, Adams' descriptions from the mounting boards appear in quotes, followed by the location of each photograph. According to the records, and unless otherwise noted, all photographs were taken in 1941 and 1942.

These are definitive photographs by Ansel Adams. They display a wider span of his work in the national parks than ever before. As Adams wrote in his proposal for the Mural Project, on August 10, 1941, "Photo-murals, because of the obvious limitations of the medium of photography, must be simpler [than paintings]—either purely decorative (such as the Screen in Secretary Ickes' office), or forcefully interpretive. I do not believe in mere big scenic enlargements, which are usually shallow in content and become tiresome in time."

As anyone can see, the photographs in the Mural Project are not shallow in content, and will not become tiresome in time. They are, as was most of the work of Ansel Adams, forcefully interpretive.

John Armor   Washington, D.C.
Peter Wright   October 1988

ANSEL ADAMS
1902-1984

Ansel Adams was born February 20, 1902, in San Francisco, California. His formal education ended in the eighth grade, but he read extensively on all subjects and was well educated as a result. He studied piano and was an accomplished concert pianist.

He took his first photograph at the age of 14 during a family vacation in Yosemite National Park. Although he was interested in photography and demonstrated some skill, it was not until 1930 that exposure to the work of older photographers, and their encouragement of his work, turned his career towards the new "art" of photography.

In the 1940's he developed the Zone System of planning the exposure of photographs, and taught that system to more than 5,000 students in seminars and workshops. His techniques are now commonly used by most teachers of photography around the world.

His 40 books, including his Autobiography that was published after his death, sold more than a million copies. Shortly before his death, he sold one of his later prints of "Moonrise, Hernandez, New Mexico," for $71,500, then the highest price ever paid for a photographic print. That photograph, and others such as "Monolith, the Face of Half Dome," are among the great artworks of the 20th century.

He was one of the founders of the photographic department at the Museum of Modern Art in New York. He helped to create the Center for Creative Photography at the University of Arizona. He started the first college department of photography at the California School of Fine Arts. And he served as a member of the Board of Trustees of the Sierra Club for 37 years.

The approach of Ansel Adams was not just to record on film the scenes that he saw. Instead, it was to visualize the scene in his mind, to take the negative to capture light at a precise moment in time, and to further refine the image in printing it. As a result, the final print was not what an observer would have seen at that time and place: it was what Adams had visualized from the beginning. His work, more than that of any other photographer in history, has caused photography to become accepted as an art form.

Ansel Adams died on April 24, 1984.

THE
GRAND
CANYON

The Grand Canyon

"Grand Canyon from the South Rim, 1941,"
Grand Canyon, Arizona.

Four billion years ago, the land that is now Arizona and several surrounding states was covered by an inland, saltwater sea. As the plates of the earth's crust moved together to form what is now North America, the water was forced out of the sea, and the Colorado River began to flow in mighty torrents out of the dense, primeval forests to the north and east of Arizona.

As the river moved it tore sand and gravel from the sedimentary rock beneath it. What had been the sea bed became the giant mesa (Spanish for table — the top surface is very flat, as the photograph shows). Over the course of two billion years, the mesa rose slowly but steadily, and as it rose the Colorado cut deeper and deeper into the rock, maintaining its course to the Pacific Ocean. It cut one canyon, leveled all in its path, and then cut a second canyon where the first had been.

Today, the Grand Canyon that was dug by the Colorado and its tributaries is a mile deep at its deepest point, and up to 18 miles wide. The Canyon is 277 miles long. The bottom layer of rock that is now exposed was deposited on that sea bed before dinosaurs walked the earth, and the advent of Homo sapiens was still 3.5 billion years in the future. The entire recorded history of mankind represents only one millionth of the time that nature took to create this wonder.

Although reduced to a shadow of its original flow, the Colorado is still a powerful river and continues to dig into the canyon floor. In another million years, the Canyon will look much like it does today.

I have come here to see the Grand Canyon of Arizona, because in that canyon Arizona has a natural wonder, which, so far as I know, is in its kind absolutely unparalleled throughout the rest of the world. I shall not attempt to describe it, because I cannot. I could not choose words that would convey. . . to any outsider what that canyon is. I want to ask you to do one thing. . . in your own interest, and in the interest of the country.

Keep this great wonder of nature as it now is.

I was delighted to learn [that] the Santa Fe Railroad [decided] not to build their hotel on the brink of the canyon. I hope you will not have a building of any kind, not a summer cottage, a hotel or anything else, to mar the wonderful grandeur, sublimity, the great loneliness and beauty of the canyon. . . .

Theodore Roosevelt, speech at the Grand Canyon, May 6, 1903, published the following day in the **New York Sun**.

You cannot improve on it; not a bit. The ages have been at work on it, and man can only mar it. What you can do is keep it for your children, your children's children and for all who come after you, as one of the great sights that every American, if he can travel at all, should see. Keep the Grand Canyon as it is.

5. *"Grand Canyon National Park from Yava Point,"* Grand Canyon, Arizona.

6. *"Grand Canyon National Park,"* Grand Canyon, Arizona.

7. *"Grand Canyon from North Rim, 1941,"* Grand Canyon, Arizona.

8.   *"Close View, Cliff Formation,"* Grand Canyon, Arizona.

9. *"Grand Canyon National Park,"* Grand Canyon, Arizona.

10.   *"Grand Canyon National Park,"* Grand Canyon, Arizona.

11. *"Grand Canyon National Park,"* Grand Canyon, Arizona.

12.   *"Grand Canyon National Park,"* Grand Canyon, Arizona.

13.   *"Grand Canyon National Park,"* Grand Canyon, Arizona.

...*When* we first became a nation, nine-tenths of the territory now included within ... the United States was wilderness. ... During the stirring and troubled years ... [before] the Revolution ... the most adventurous hunters, the vanguard of the hardy army of pioneer settlers, first crossed the Alleghanies, and roamed far and wide through the lonely, danger-haunted forests which filled the No-man's-land between the Tennessee and the Ohio ....

While the first Continental Congress was still sitting, Daniel Boone, the archetype of the American hunter, was leading his bands of tall backwoods riflemen to settle in the beautiful country of Kentucky, where the red and white warriors strove with such obstinate rage that both races alike grew to know it as "the dark and bloody ground."

Theodore Roosevelt, "The American Wilderness: Wilderness Hunters and Wilderness Game," **The Wilderness Hunter**, G. P. Putnam's Sons, New York, 1893.

Boone and his fellow-hunters were the heralds of the oncoming civilization, the pioneers in that conquest of the wilderness which has ... been practically achieved in our own day. Where they pitched their camps and built their log huts ..., towns grew up, and ... tillers of the soil ... thronged in .... Then, ill-at-ease among the settlements for which they had ... made ready the way ... the restless hunters moved onward .... Their untamable souls ever found something congenial and beyond measure attractive in the lawless freedom of the lives of the very savages against whom they warred so bitterly.

[The national forests, unlike the national parks, were intended for responsible, renewable uses, such as timbering, grazing, homesteading, etc. In the same address, President Roosevelt asked for expansion of Yellowstone, acceptance of Yosemite as a gift from California, and creation of new parks on the Canyon of the Colorado River, and among the redwood forests of California. Although the acceptance of Carlsbad Caverns into the System came long after Roosevelt's presidency, it was entirely consistent with his policies.]

15. *"Grand Canyon National Park,"* Grand Canyon, Arizona.

THE INDIANS
OF THE
SOUTHWEST

The Indians
of the Southwest

"Navajo Woman and Child, Canyon de Chelly, Arizona,"
Canyon de Chelly, Arizona.

Among the most evocative relics of the Indians of the American Southwest are the cliff dwellings of the Anasazi. The largest of these structures is in the Canyon de Chelly, near the Arizona-New Mexico border, and is known popularly as the White House.

This structure was built in a cleft in a south-facing cliff beginning about 2,400 years ago. It is constructed primarily of sun-fired adobe bricks, and at its height it contained the homes, and tribal and ceremonial buildings, for about 1,000 residents throughout the Canyon. Anasazi means "the Ancient Ones."

The best current estimate as to why the Anasazi abandoned their homes and died out about 700 years ago is changes in climate that turned the Southwest from forest land to semi-arid and desert areas. A constant supply of timber was needed both for construction and repairs, as well as firewood. With the change in climate, a necessary product to maintain life in this city was gone.

Note that the Anasazi erected a sign outside their city. On the face of the cliff below the White House are two pictographs, one showing a man, the other a bird, the Arizona roadrunner.

The Indians that Ansel Adams photographed are Navaho and Pueblo. They have lived in this area thousands of years, presently on reservations in Arizona, New Mexico, and Colorado.

Today, there are about 175,000 Navaho Indians, some still maintaining their distinctive villages and tribal customs. Prior to contact with the white man, there were about three times as many.

Other major tribes living in or near the national parks of the Southwest are the Hopi, the Zuni, the Pueblo, the Apache, the Utes, and the Paiutes. The Cherokee are the only tribe in the area who are not native to it. They were driven by the U.S. Army from their homes in the Blue Ridge Mountains on the "Trail of Tears" in 1838, where many of them died.

The man should have youth and strength who seeks adventure in the wide, waste spaces of the earth, in the marshes, and among the vast mountain masses, in the northern forests, amid the steaming jungles of the tropics, or on the deserts of sand or of snow. . . . But much, very much, remains for the man who has "warmed both hands before the fire of life," and who, although he loves the great cities, loves even more the fenceless grassland, and the forest-clad hills.

The grandest scenery of the world is his to look at if he chooses; and he can witness the strange ways of the tribes who have survived into an alien age from an immemorial past, tribes whose priests dance in honor of the wolf and the bear.

Theodore Roosevelt, "The Joy of the Wild," preface to A Book-Lover's Holidays in the Open, Charles Scribner's Sons, New York, 1916.

21. *"Canyon de Chelly,"* Canyon de Chelly, Arizona.

22. *"Navaho Woman and Infant, Canyon de Chelly, Arizona,"* Canyon de Chelly, Arizona.

23.   *"Cliff Palace, Mesa Verde National Park,"* Mesa Verde, Colorado.

24. *"Flock in Owens Valley, 1941,"* Owens Valley, California.

25. *"Cliff Palace, Mesa Verde National Park,"* Mesa Verde, Colorado.

26. *"Dance, San Ildefonso Pueblo, New Mexico, 1942,"* San Ildefonso Pueblo, New Mexico.

27. *"Untitled,"* Mesa Verde National Park, Colorado.

28. *"Mesa Verde National Park, 1941,"* Mesa Verde, Colorado.

29. *"Church, Taos Pueblo, New Mexico, 1942,"* Taos Pueblo, New Mexico.

30.   *"Dance, San Ildefonso Pueblo, New Mexico, 1942,"* San Ildefonso Pueblo, New Mexico.

31. *"Cliff Palace, Mesa Verde National Park,"* Mesa Verde, Colorado.

32. *"Church, Acoma Pueblo,"* Acoma Pueblo, New Mexico

33. *"Acoma Pueblo, New Mexico,"* Acoma Pueblo, New Mexico.

34.   *"Navaho Girl, Canyon de Chelly, Arizona,"* Canyon de Chelly, Arizona.

35.   *"Church, Acoma Pueblo,"* Acoma Pueblo, New Mexico.

Southwest of the Rockies evil and terrible deserts stretch for leagues and leagues, mere waterless wastes of sandy plain and barren mountain, broken here and there by narrow strips of fertile ground. Rain rarely falls, and there are no clouds to dim the brazen sun. The rivers run in deep canyons, or are swallowed by the burning sand; the smaller watercourses are dry throughout the greater part of the year.

Beyond this desert region rise the sunny Sierras of California, with their flower-clad slopes and groves of giant trees; and north of them, along the coast, the rain shrouded mountain chains of Oregon and Washington, matted with the towering growth of the mighty evergreen forest. . . .

Zoologically speaking, the north temperate zones of the Old and New Worlds are very similar, differing from one another much less than they do from the various regions south of them, or than those regions differ among themselves. The untrodden American wilderness resembles both in game and physical character the forests, the mountains, and the steppes of the Old World as it was at the beginning of our era.

Theodore Roosevelt, "The American Wilderness: Wilderness Hunters and Wilderness Game," **The Wilderness Hunter**, *G. P. Putnam's Sons, New York, 1893.*

37. *"Walpi, Arizona, 1941,"* Walpi, Arizona.

YELLOWSTONE
NATIONAL PARK

Yellowstone
National Park

"Old Faithful Geyser, Yellowstone National Park,"
Yellowstone, Wyoming.

Established by Act of Congress on March 1, 1872, Yellowstone was the first national park ever created. Because of its extraordinary scenery, geology, wildlife, and recreational possibilities, it was easy for Congress to see that this resource should be preserved for future generations. Even so, there were some members who argued that it was not a proper use of public funds to purchase and operate national parks.

One of Yellowstone's most interesting features is Old Faithful, the geyser that erupts every 78 minutes.

Although the Rangers set a clock to let visitors prepare for the next eruption, in fact its timing has changed by as much as 22 minutes on a daily basis.

When creation of Yellowstone was under consideration, residents of nearby Wyoming towns objected to the idea, believing that hunting and recreation opportunities, and therefore tourist business, would be diminished by the park. Since that time, in communities around Yellowstone and other parks, citizens have discovered that well-run parks are both good neighbors and good for business.

Every... *lover of nature, every man who appreciates the majesty and beauty of the wilderness and of wild life, should strike hands with the far-sighted men who wish to preserve our material resources, in the effort to keep our forests and our game beasts, game-birds, and game-fish — indeed, all the living creatures of prairie and woodland and seashore — from wanton destruction.*

It is entirely in our power as a nation to preserve large tracts of wilderness ... as playgrounds for the rich and poor alike, and to preserve the game so it shall continue to exist for the benefit of all lovers of nature.... But this end can only be achieved by wise laws and by a resolute enforcement of those laws. Lack of such legislation and enforcement will result in harm to all of us, but most of all in harm to the nature-lover who does not possess vast wealth.

Theodore Roosevelt, "Wilderness Reserves: The Yellowstone Park," in **Outdoor Pastimes of an American Hunter,** *Charles Scribner's Sons, New York, 1905.*

43.   *"Fountain Geyser Pool, Yellowstone National Park,"* Yellowstone, Wyoming.

44.   *"Jupiter Terrace — Fountain Geyser Pool, Yellowstone National Park,"* Yellowstone, Wyoming.

45. *"Yellowstone Falls,"* Yellowstone, Wyoming.

46.   *"Firehold River, Yellowstone National Park,"* Yellowstone, Wyoming.

47. *"Castle Geyser Cone, Yellowstone National Park,"* Yellowstone, Wyoming.

48. *"Old Faithful Geyser, Yellowstone National Park,"* Yellowstone, Wyoming. (All of these photographs are part of a study of Old Faithful, taken at various angles, to capture the changing patterns of light.)

49. *"Old Faithful Geyser, Yellowstone National Park,"* Yellowstone, Wyoming.

50. *"The Fishing Cone — Yellowstone Lake, Yellowstone National Park,"* Yellowstone, Wyoming.

51. *"Fountain Geyser Pool, Yellowstone National Park,"* Yellowstone, Wyoming.

52. *"Yellowstone Lake — Hot Springs Overflow, Yellowstone National Park,"* Yellowstone, Wyoming.

53. *"Central Geyser Basin, Yellowstone National Park,"* Yellowstone, Wyoming.

Most *of us, as we grow older, grow to care relatively less for sport than for the splendid freedom and abounding health of the outdoor life in the woods, on the plains, and among the great mountains; and to the true nature-lover it is melancholy to see the wilderness stripped of the wild creatures that gave it no small part of its peculiar charm. It is inevitable and probably necessary that the wolf and the cougar should go; but the bighorn and white goat among the rocks, the blacktail and wapiti feeding in the sedgy ponds — these add beyond measure to the wilderness landscape, and if they are taken away they leave a lack which nothing else can quite make good. So it is of those true birds of the wilderness, the eagle and the raven, and, indeed, of all the wild things, furred, feathered and finned.*

Theodore Roosevelt, "The Wapiti or Round-Horned Elk," from **Outdoor Pastimes of an American Hunter,** Charles Scribner's Sons, New York, 1905.

55. *"Yellowstone Lake, Mt. Sheridan,"* Yellowstone, Wyoming.

CARLSBAD CAVERNS

Carlsbad Caverns

*"Formations, along trail in the Big Room,
beyond the Temple of the Sun,"*
Carlsbad Caverns, New Mexico.

Carlsbad Caverns, among the largest in the world, were discovered in the early 1900s by a guano miner. They were declared a National Monument in 1923. In 1930 they were taken into the National Park System.

Carlsbad Caverns have not yet been fully explored. They contain at least 21.7 miles of passageways, and hundreds of rooms. The largest room is the Chamber Room, or Big Room, the third largest underground room known in the world. It is 1.5 miles long by 250 feet high, with a floor area of 14 acres. The entire U.S. Capitol would fit in this room without touching the walls or ceiling.

The formation of the Caverns began about 250 million years ago, after limestone had been laid down as the floor of an ancient sea. When the surface rose to become dry land, semitropical forests grew above it, and rushing rivers dug into gaps in the surface, gradually eating away the rooms of the Caverns.

When the forests disappeared above, trickles of water remained running in the empty rooms. These trickles redeposited limestone in stalactites hanging from the ceilings, and stalagmites rising from the floor. The largest stalagmite ever discovered, the Giant Dome, is located here. It took approximately 60 million years for trickles of mineral-laden water to create this formation.

The forest reserve policy can be successful only when it has the full support of the people of the West. It cannot safely, and should not in any case, be imposed upon them against their will. But neither can we accept the views of those whose only interest in the forest is temporary; who are anxious to reap what they have not sown and then move away, leaving desolation behind them. On the contrary, it is everywhere and always the interest of the permanent settler and the permanent businessman, the man with a stake in the country, which must be considered and which must decide.

*President Theodore Roosevelt, Fourth Annual Message to the Senate and House of Representatives, Volume XIV, **Messages & Papers of the Presidents**, December 6, 1904, published by the Bureau of National Literature, New York, 1912.*

61.   *"The Giant Dome, largest stalagmite thus far discovered. It is 16 feet in diameter and estimated to be 60 million years old. Hall of Giants, Big Room,"* Carlsbad, New Mexico.

62. *"The Rock of Ages, Big Room,"* Carlsbad, New Mexico.

63. *"Formations, a few of the many natural formations at Carlsbad Caverns,"* Carlsbad, New Mexico.

64.   *"The large stalagmite formations and the onyx drapes above it, in the King's Palace,"* Carlsbad, New Mexico.

65.   *"The Giant Domes in the interior of Carlsbad Caverns,"* Carlsbad, New Mexico.

66. *"Formations, stalagmites in the Queen's Chamber,"* Carlsbad, New Mexico.

67. *"In the Queen's Chamber,"* Carlsbad, New Mexico.

THE
NATIONAL
PARKS

The National Parks

"Grand Teton,"
Grand Teton National Park, Wyoming.

The first public areas created and maintained by Acts of Congress were "national monuments," not "parks." The first was a statue of Washington, in 1783. In 1790 the first park-like area was preserved by Congress in the "monument" category — the Naval Live Oaks Reservation, in Florida.

The first "national park" created and owned by the United States was Yellowstone, in 1872. By 1916, eight years after President Teddy Roosevelt had left office, there were about five million of acres of national parks and monuments. But each had to fight for its own annual appropriations, and there was no coherent national policy concerning the parks.

As a private citizen, Roosevelt continued to campaign for a National Park Service, and in 1916 it was created. Urged on by Roosevelt and many others of like mind, Congress finally concluded that national parks were not just a luxury or decoration, but rather an integral part of our national heritage and national life.

By 1941, when Ansel Adams began work on the Mural Project, there were 21.6 million acres of national parks, in a total of 164 facilities, with an annual operating budget of $5,242,000, and 21 million visitors annually. The comparable figures in 1988 are 80.0 million acres, 350 facilities, and a budget of $744.9 million, for the benefit of 300 million visitors annually.

The American people have been gradually awakened during the past few years to the idea of a city park as not merely an adornment, but as an instrument of social service to the community. . . . But we have not yet . . .applied the same idea to our National parks. It is true we have an ample measure of them in area, but we are not yet sure as a people just what we want them for; and we have as yet given them no efficient and intelligent administration. [We have] . . .thirteen National parks, embracing over four and a half million acres. At present . . .each is a separate. . . unit for administrative purposes. Special appropriations are made for each park, and the employment of a common supervising and directing force is impossible.

A bill is before Congress for the creation of a Bureau of National Parks . . . [to] have the supervision, management and control of all the National parks and monuments in the country, and. . . the duty of developing those areas. . . [to] promote public recreation and public health through their use by the people. We have a single amendment to propose. . . . The new bureau should be called the National Park Service. . . . The establishment of a National Park service is justified by considerations of good administration, of the value of natural beauty as a National asset, and of the effectiveness of outdoor life and recreation in the production of good citizenship.

Theodore Roosevelt, **The Outlook**, February 3, 1912.

73. *"The Tetons — Snake River,"* Grand Teton National Park, Wyoming.

74. *"In Glacier National Park,"* Glacier National Park, Montana.

75.   *"Rocky Mountain National Park, Never Summer Range,"* Rocky Mountain National Park, Colorado.

76. *"Untitled,"* Grand Canyon National Park, Arizona.

77.   *"In Glacier National Park,"* Glacier National Park, Montana.

78. *"Saguaros, Saguaro National Monument,"* Saguaro National Monument, Arizona.

79. *"In Rocky Mountain National Park,"* Rocky Mountain National Park, Colorado.

The conservation of our natural resources and their proper use constitute the fundamental problem of our National life. We must maintain for our civilization the adequate material basis without which that civilization cannot exist. . . . There must be a realization of the fact that to waste, to destroy, our natural resources, to skim and exhaust the land instead of using it to increase its usefulness, will result in undermining in the days of our children the very prosperity which we ought by right to hand down to them amplified and developed.

President Theodore Roosevelt, Seventh Annual Message to the Senate and House of Representatives, Volume XIV, **Messages & Papers of the Presidents**, December 3, 1907, published by the Bureau of National Literature, New York, 1912.

81.   *"Boulder Dam, 1941,"* Boulder Dam, Colorado.

82. *"Acoma Pueblo,"* Acoma Pueblo, New Mexico.

83.   *"Boulder Dam, 1941,"* Boulder Dam, Colorado.

84. *"North Palisade from Windy Point,"* Kings River Canyon, California.

85. *"Heaven's Peak,"* Glacier National Park, Montana.

86. *"Mt. Moran and Jackson Lake from Signal Hill, Teton National Park,"* Grand Teton National
Park, Wyoming.

87. *"Canyon de Chelly,"* Canyon de Chelly, Arizona.

I *was a very near-sighted small boy, and did not even know that my eyes were not normal until I was fourteen; and so my field studies up to that point were even more worthless than those of the average boy who "collects" natural history specimens much as he collects stamps. . . . Just before my fourteenth birthday my father started me on my. . . career as a naturalist by giving me a pair of spectacles, a French pin-fire double-barrelled shotgun — and lessons in stuffing birds. The spectacles literally opened a new world to me. The mechanism of the pin-fire gun was without springs, and therefore could not get out of order — an important point as my mechanical ability was nil. The lessons in. . . mounting birds were given to me by Mr. John G. Bell . . . who had accompanied Audubon on his trip to the then "far West. . . ."*

One cold and snowy winter. . . at Garrison-on-the-Hudson. . . I spied a flock of crossbills in a pine, fired, and excitedly rushed forward. A twig caught my spectacles and snapped them I know not

Theodore Roosevelt, "My Life as a Naturalist," **American Museum Journal**, May 1918.

where. . . . I could still make out the red birds lying in the snow; and. . . I abandoned all thought of my glasses and began a near-sighted hunt for my quarry. . . . I lost all trace of my glasses; my day's sport — or scientific endeavor. . . — came to an abrupt end; and as a result I never again in my life went out shooting, whether after sparrows or elephants, without a spare pair of spectacles in my pocket. After some ranch experiences I had my spectacle cases made of steel which saved my life in after-years when a man shot into me in Milwaukee.

89. *"In Glacier National Park,"* Glacier National Park, Montana.

90. *"In Rocky Mountain National Park,"* Rocky Mountain National Park, Colorado.

91. *"Tetons from Signal Mountain,"* Grand Teton National Park, Wyoming.

92.   *"Junction Peak,"* Kings River Canyon, California.

93. *"In Saguaro National Monument,"* Saguaro National Monument, Arizona.

94.   *"Long's Peak from North, Rocky Mountain National Park,"* Rocky Mountain National Park, Colorado.

95. *"In Glacier National Park,"* Glacier National Park, Montana.

At Plain Dealing many birds nest within a stone's throw of the rambling, attractive house, with its numerous outbuildings, old garden, orchard, and venerable locusts and catalpas. Among them were Baltimore and orchard orioles, purple grackles, flickers, and red-headed woodpeckers, bluebirds, robins, king-birds, and indigo-buntings. One observation which I made was of real interest. On May 18, 1907, I saw a small party of passenger-pigeons, birds I had not seen for a quarter of a century and never expected to see again.

I saw them two or three times flying hither and thither with great rapidity, and once they perched in a tall dead pine on the edge of an old field. They were unmistakable; yet the sight was so unexpected that I almost doubted my eyes, and I welcomed a bit of corroborative evidence coming from

Theodore Roosevelt, "Small Country Neighbors,"
Scribner's Magazine, October 1907.

Dick, the colored foreman at Plain Dealing. Dick is a frequent companion of mine in rambles around the country, and he is an unusually close and accurate observer of birds, and of wild things generally.

97. *"Grand Teton,"* Grand Teton National Park, Wyoming.

98. *"From Going-to-the-Sun Chalet, Glacier National Park,"* Glacier National Park, Montana.

99. *"In Rocky Mountain National Park,"* Rocky Mountain National Park, Colorado.

100. *"Roaring River, Kings Region,"* Kings River Canyon, California.

101.   *"Near Death Valley,"* Death Valley National Monument, California.

102. *"St. Mary's Lake, Glacier National Park,"* Glacier National Park, Montana.

103. *"Near Teton National Park,"* Grand Teton National Park, Wyoming.

104. *"In Glacier National Park,"* Glacier National Park, Montana.

105. *"In Rocky Mountain National Park,"* Rocky Mountain National Park, Colorado.

106. *"Clouds — White Pass,"* Kings River Canyon, California.

107. *"Kearsarge Pinnacles,"* Kings River Canyon, California.

The *beauty and charm of the wilderness are his for the asking, for the edges of the wilderness lie close beside the beaten roads of present travel. He can see the red splendor of desert sunsets, the unearthly glory of the after-glow on the battlements of desolate mountains. In the sapphire gulfs of oceans he can visit islets, above which the wings of myriads of sea-fowl make a kind of shifting cuneiform script in the air. He can ride along the brink of the stupendous cliff-walled canyon, where eagles soar below him, and cougars make their lairs on the ledges and harry the big-horned sheep. He can journey through northern forests, the home of the giant moose, the forests of fragrant and murmuring life in the summer, the iron-bound and melancholy forests of winter.*

The joy of living is his who has the heart to demand it.

Theodore Roosevelt, "The Joy of the Wild," preface to *A Book-Lover's Holidays in the Open*, Charles Scribner's Sons, New York, 1916.

109.   *"Evening, McDonald Lake, Glacier National Park,"* Glacier National Park, Montana.

INDEX OF PHOTOGRAPHS

* These are the reference numbers for the Mural Project photographs in the National Archives, Washington, D.C.

** These photographs were taken in Kings River Canyon in 1936, which was at that time proposed as a national park. They were supplied by Ansel Adams to the Department of Interior as part of his fulfillment of the contract for the Mural Project.

For anyone with an interest in the writings of Theodore Roosevelt, *Theodore Roosevelt, Wilderness Writings*, edited and with an introduction by Paul Schullery (Peregrine Smith Books, Salt Lake City, 1986) is highly recommended.